NOT TOO LATE FOR LOVING

A Lifetime Of Occasional Verses

Graham Tayar

GRAHAM TAYAR

Illustrations by James Foot
Camel cover by Richard Williams
Calligraphy by John Nash
Cottage by Robin Penna

SMALLER SKY BOOKS

First published in Great Britain in 2000

by

Smaller Sky Books
217 Woodstock Road
Oxford OX2 7AD
United Kingdom

www.smallerskybooks.co.uk

ISBN 1 903100 02 X

Produced by

The Short Run Book Company Ltd
St Stephen's House
Arthur Road
Windsor
SL4 1RY
United Kingdom

NOT TOO LATE FOR LOVING

A Lifetime of Occasional Verses
(1956-1999)

At the age of sixty-six, this is my first collection of poems and indeed may be my only one unless my life or productivity changes dramatically (though I have written twenty in the last twelve months or so).

In retrospect, I detect no overarching principles or themes, except my occasional propensity for falling in love and reflecting this in verse. Many of them are meant to be light; most are short, rhyme and even scan.

I suppose that having at odd and unexpected moments felt the need to express myself in verse, my wish for their survival (and for others to see them) has done the rest. I hope readers will find among them some poems that they enjoy; a few might gain from being read aloud.

They are presented in more or less chronological order and comprise virtually the entire output of my writing lifetime.

Some have previously been printed in *ENVOI, EXTRA VERSE, POETRY AND AUDIENCE, POETRY AND AUDIENCE ANTHOLOGY, TRIBUNE, TRIO, HOT NEWS, ENDELLION NOTES, BIRMINGHAM POST*, as part of letters in *ENCOUNTER* and *THE LISTENER*, in the literary biography *JOHN WAIN: A MAN OF LETTERS*, and broadcast on *RADIO SRI LANKA*. Some were read at *PICCADILLY POETS*. A few were *NEW STATESMAN* or *SPECTATOR* competition entries, or verses that failed the *LITERARY REVIEW* test course. However, waste not......

I am particularly grateful to Douglas Hill for suggesting the title and printing some of them in *TRIBUNE* when he was Literary Editor, to Beatrice McCartney for typing them, and to my friends the painter James Foot for his splendid illustrations, calligrapher John Nash for his elegant lettering, printer and illustrator Robin Penna for the drawing of my cottage where many were written, and the distinguished animator (and jazz trumpeter) Richard Williams, for his brilliant interpretation of *A CAMEL TROUVÉ*.

They are dedicated, of course, to M., L., P., J., C. and Catherine Raeburn, which is as it should be.

GT, December 1999

N.B. The first ten verses were written in Birmingham, the next three in Ethiopia, and the rest in London, Wales, Cornwall, Spain, Greece and Sri Lanka.

CONTENTS

WRITERS' CRAMP – HALFWAY THROUGH ACT THREE

My hero stands dumb,
His arms outspread
Words do not come.

The tension is broken
All feeling numb
His last speech unspoken.

The edges of sleep
– My boredom a token –
Round the red eyes creep.

No power in my head
To laugh or to weep,
The play is dead.

1957

CLIMBERS

For Maynard Tweed

Some find in rocks
A kind of peace.
Their trust casts out
The fear of falling.

But others less
Secure in faith
Experience
Each climb as death.

The former often
Fall and die.
The others live
To die again.

1957

ITS OWN REWARD

Let those who live quite virtuously
Forget the error and the doubt;
For them the flames are soon put out.

There is no biting burning rage
For those who live most virtuously
Measure their progress page by page.

The passion and the pain of love
Are concepts they have grown above,
All those who live so virtuously.

1957

LIKE THE LORD PRIVY SEAL

When on a train, my penchant I must curb
For pointing out the rose-bay willow herb,
And telling those in range it's all baloney,
Not willow, rose nor bay, an utter phoney !

1957

SOHO

Evening Standard, Tuesday, 22 November 1994. *Derek Nimmo was in nostalgic mood. "My first home after I married was in Old Compton Street, just by L'Escargot. Jack Spot (Comer) was the hood running Soho at the time. This was before the Krays and there were nice hoods who just had razors."*

Match me this marvel, save in Comer's time;
A bloodstained village half as old as crime.

1956

{A New Statesman competition entry – verse on town or village – which was commended. See p.109 for my next entry, forty years on, which won – though admittedly so did sixteen other entries.}

SONG FOR A YOUNG MAN

You there, boy, with love-lorn gait,
Sixteen perhaps but old enough
For love. Why do you stand and wait
On a half-lit corner for your love ?

Perhaps she's gone; or never came.
The boy next door who carried her books
Decoyed her away. His little game
Was to gaze in her eyes, at her long deep looks.

The way of a woman's mind is hard
To grasp for your quick and youthful lust,
And harder still the way to her heart
When your body's fire she has turned to dust.

You there, boy, you'll understand,
Though the hard earth crumbles, there's time enough.
But nothing now to do but stand
On a half-lit corner for your love.

1958

STRANGE MAN TO LITTLE GIRL

That way lies the wood. A tangled quilt
Made from forgotten patterns. Dark, although
In places lonely buttons of light
Fasten it to the empty sky.
Child, there is no place unsafe for pure
And innocent adventurers. Yet wait,
The cunning sounds weave one thin curtain
Which shuts out the certain danger,
Hides whisperingly the menace of the wood.
Perhaps tomorrow I shall walk with you.
No harm should come when I who know
Each curious glade decide to walk with you
Under the full moon, child. See in your mind
The delicate lace edges of the trees,
And the white star holes.
Tomorrow, child, under the ripe full moon,
But secretly, that those who may distrust
My mind's wild kingdom, do not meddle.
Tomorrow, then, child.

1958

OLD MAN'S SONG

In my innocence I craved
Love's raptures from a passing whore.
But soon I learnt that payment made
For love bought less and cost me more.

Much later, in my middle years,
I sought and found a settled bed.
In arrogance that time confers
I misused love until love fled.

My spendthrift passion led my will
On love's account to overdraw,
And now in age I vainly still
Pursue my loving from a whore.

1958

PHALLIC FRAGMENT

In a high tower, my loving passion lies;
The earth's vibrations make its ramparts shake.
Then, when it moves, and cracks, and falls, and dies
The course of love has caused its core to break.

1958

BLOCK

The page is blank, a record truly kept
To illustrate cerebral impotence,
The mind awhirl with symbols, yet inept
At catching them, reducing signs to sense.

Hands poised as though to snatch from empty air
The hidden key whose touch can open wide
The treasury of skill, the untouched layer
Of image, rhyme and rhythm side by side.

But to reduce it to a single phrase,
The urge to write outruns accomplishment,
A hesitant anxiety betrays
The search for meaning when the words are spent.

1958

THERE IS A MOMENT

For M

There is a moment when control is lost,
When shadows turn to faces, and the light
Yields to the heart's dark probings. Troubled sight
Is forced to turn within. Love counts the cost.

This is the moment, in between the folds
Of sleep and waking, when the tired mind
Is trapped. The instinct to escape behind
The screen of work or dreams no longer holds.

At last the image and the wish are one.
Whatever was the object and the prize
Has no more value. Now the heart decries
The doubtful gains when payment has begun.

This is the moment when control is lost.
Whose love's departed, he will count the cost.

Addis Ababa, 1961

TIME TO GO

There were many;
Mothers who comforted their children,
And children, cold and frightened, who were
  comforted;
Men who had cheated and lied, grasped at success,
And those whose lives were honourable, bearing no
  disgrace.
Others, older, already half-emptied of greed, passion
  and lust,
Waited with milder apprehension for what in any case
Was soon to be theirs by right of seniority.

There were few;
Children of mothers, grandfathers of children,
Shaping the world, resolved and intent
On saving its soul, whatever the cost,
From fates worse than death and leukaemia.
Their consciences led them, and as their reward
For the years of service, the nights of doubt,
A job well done, even to the end.

And then there were none.

Addis Ababa, 1961

*But fortunately it never happened, though the coming of a
nuclear holocaust seemed real enough to those of us who were
young in the early 1960s.*

A CRUCIFIXION

For Gabre Christos Desta, whose painting
had real nails protruding through the Cross

From Fra Angelico to Dali,
  The ritual sacrifice has been
  A peg to hang a picture on.

Jesus, limp and elegant,
  Stares patiently from stone or paint
  A promise of eternal bliss.

The tortured body of Calvary
  (or Auschwitz or Hiroshima)
  Does not unpleasantly intrude.

But here a different lesson's told,
  For jagged metal nails tear
  Through the canvas and the flesh.
That truth's as final as we'll know.
  The gifts that God bestowed on man
  Were hatred, hunger, pain and death.

Addis Ababa, 1963

SUDDENLY WITH SURPRISE

For L

Suddenly with surprise it seems
That we have weathered the first storms
And entered for a time more peaceful waters
With our rigging still intact.

There have been perils, and lesser irritations,
Bouts of seasickness, surfeits of rum,
Often times when it seemed
Living was less dangerous ashore.

Maybe it is; and perhaps other ships
Had more grace, carried finer passengers,
Certainly boasted richer cargoes. But ours
Has grown stronger against the elements.

Now neither sea nor storm can shake her;
As long as our compass holds, she should
Ride true and with fair winds find
Ports that shall astonish us both.

1968

ONE TYPE OF AMBIGUITY

A British tourist quickly finds
That US fannies are behinds.
But here its meaning's contrapuntal:
Our fannies are full female frontal.

1972

BENEFIT OF CLERGY

(A Kerry, not a Limerick)

A transvesticist from Tralee
Would seduce any cleric she'd see.
Expectant young vicars
Laid hands on her knickers
But found to their cost she was he.

1972

A LIMERICK OF UNRESOLVED ALTERNATIVES

An average young lad or old man,
Whether tall or short, black, white or tan,
Whatever he's doing,
Either wanking or wooing,
May soon find that he can't – or he can.

1972

UNOFFICIAL ANNIVERSARY

For P

Birthdays passing no more show
A child's delight in living slow.
This day itself can only measure
Time; we seek a longer pleasure
Held in memory and giving,
Snatched amidst our daily living.
Counting hours, not years, we test
Our little life against the rest.
But holding fast to what we have,
Our lunchtime calendar of love.

1975

WEEKEND COTTAGE

The cottage lies hard against the road.
The tourists sail past our window
Some beating a passage into our reluctant living-
room
As though it were a natural extension
Of the harbour and the car park.
The natives are friendly. They smile
And smile, awaiting the autumn retreat.
When winter comes, will they still smile ?
Will we be tourists or natives then ?
And who will decide whether the cottage
Belongs to us, or that we have merely
Let it to ourselves for a Christmas holiday ?

Port Isaac, 1976

NO. 17 MIDDLE STREET, PORT ISAAC

No Dollery, no Hollies,
No trams, no Snow Hill station.
Kardomah, Woodman, Institute
Have passed beyond cremation.

The ashes all are scattered
The lovers all are gone
The clocks have ceased their chiming,
Only the shades live on.

1976

But it was always like this in Birmingham. As the first verse of an anonymous popular song of 1828 put it:

Full twenty years and more are past
Since I left Brummagem.
But I set out for home at last
To good old Brummagem.

But every place is altered so
There's hardly a single place I know
And it fills my heart with grief and woe
That I can't find Brummagem.

BIRDS IN CRETE

Some, they say, live here
All the year round,
Like the cuck without a coo
Which counterpoints every complex chorus
With a certain simplicity.

But the rest have just arrived
(they say). Last week was quiet.
Until overnight, a swirling of wings,
Then furled after flight,
Birds producing their patchwork quilt
Of African sounds,
And soon a temporary affection
For Europe, England and the soft south-east.

Who decides the time to go ?
Who stays over, and who goes on ?
And who will settle for Hampstead Heath or head
   firmly
Northwards on more Arctic routes ?
Do they draw lots ? Have mass meetings ?
Vote at each crosswind whether to curve or scatter
Or fly straight away from the sun ?
It all seems far beyond the bounds
Of human reason or computer's skill.

Yet the birds all seem to know
When to stay and where to go,
As year by year and century by century
They blend the magic of certainty
With the certainty of magic.

Crete, 1982

XANIA AT DAWN

Why XANIA ? Well, transcribed,
There are far too many versions
To make it easy. Chania, Hania,
Canea, even Khania – each
A linguistic approximation
(only the Greek is true),
A trace of past intruders,
Like the dead mosques
– some were once churches, others became them –
All now most desolate, unattached minarets
Marking nothing, except centuries
Of an alien culture, long gone away.
Or like most of the rest, absorbed without notice.

For consider the peoples and conquests of Crete.
First the Kydonian and the Minoan,
Then Dorian, geometric, Roman and Byzantine,
Arab, Venetian, Genoese and Turk.
Last and least the Third Reich Germans
(soon hurriedly departing). But always
The Cretans remained, with language, church,
And a sense of freedom.
Only the Greek is true.

Now, standing on the harbour wall
(all the boats idle, all the town still),
At first Sunday light, with the slanted sun
Rising watchfully over crescent and campanile,
And the snow-topped mountains looming behind,

I somehow am filled with the sense of
This living museum of Europe's past,
And I share its warmth, echo its sounds,
Encompass its history
In overwhelming morning joy.

Crete, 1982

AFTER LOVE

For L

Love as it passes
Leaves some regret
Just as the past is
A sun not quite set.

Yet in its passing
We lose only part.
What stays is the last thing
Left in the heart.

For love's no brief songbird
To pass before night.
It lingers, though half-heard,
As long as there's light.

So now undertaking
To store what won't mend,
What's left from our breaking
May last to the end.

1982

HOLDING

For C

Time enough has passed for me
To feel my longing still runs true.
And if it holds for you, then we
 – taking on trust a longer view –

Should bind our futures, hold our course,
Make plans, build castles in the air,
And conjure up through some dark force
A dream quite magical and fair.

But being in love's a transient mix
Of bodies, minds and hearts held fast.
The skill's not starting, but to fix
Our passing pleasures in harder cast.

So half a continent away,
I see you plain at each day's start,
And hold you with me all the day
To carve your beauty in my heart.

Crete, 1982

ALL THE THINGS YOU ARE

For C

You are the punctuation to my days,
The still sharp focus around which I turn,
The sign which leads down unexpected ways,
The golden prize whose joy I hope to earn.

You are the time when past and future meet,
An island of my life in unknown seas,
A loving sanctuary, a last retreat
To make me safe and thaw me when I freeze.

You are these things and more; for what you give
Has warmed the whole cold world in which I live.

1982

THREE VIEWS OF THE FALKLAND WAR

1. A SONNET OF PATRIOTIC DISORIENTATION

On holiday, one ought to take things easy
Not catching newscasts, chasing British papers.
In Crete, such frenzy gives my friends the vapours
While Haig and Pym in Greek make me quite queasy.

I know that there are those whose every particle
Is pleased to fight an Argentine Armada.
But while confused, I really find it harder
To see all this as warlike and not farcical.

Somehow out here, one's not disposed to worry
Although their fleet and ours are on their mettle.
It would cost less for Falkland's folk to settle
Well-subsidized in Wiltshire, say, or Surrey.

I cannot help but feel there's some mistake
When Thatcher sees herself as Francis Drake.

Crete, 16 April 1982

2. FOOTNOTE

Now being home a day or two,
I've quickly formed another view.
I've caught the patriotic mood
I'm banning Argentinian food.

I'm quite prepared to fight – I think –
At least to the last drop of ink.
And if we win, a poem I'll forge
For Margaret, England and St George.

London, 23 April 1982

3. DELAYED POSTSCRIPT

But then I had to stop
because of the sudden horror,
the blood-stream which washed out the jokes
with the lives that were wasted.

Yet despite the Belgrano, the mock heroics,
the surge of cheap euphoria, the doubtful glory,
the memory still sings of real heroes,
necessary sacrifice, a sense of country
and not-so-empty gestures.

Later, long after, when the headlines are faded,
the bodies buried and the sadness muted,
some things – for a lifetime – are remembered:
Goose Green, counting them out and back,
the battle of Max Hastings,
and the times – sometimes –
when our spirits were lifted,
and some – perhaps – of our enemies – perhaps –
were – perhaps – deterred.

So when farce turns to tragedy,
both are graven in history;
for even small wars cast long shadows
behind them.

London, May 1987

COUNTRY MATTERS

I have an aunt in old Baghdad
Whose friends and neighbours think her mad.
For every Sunday at eleven,
She makes her personal pact with Heaven,
Rotates her prayer book till it falls
In line by compass with St Paul's.
By borrowing from Islamic lore
She underlines thus even more
That when in countries Asiatic
It's meet – and safer – for pragmatic
Anglicans to change their view,
Cherish the old, adapt the new;
And so empirically she shows
What every wise expatriate knows:
Though east is east, and west is west,
A modest compromise is best.

1982

GENESIS

For Daryl at 15

At a blow, you've written
Seven poems in a day;
Such a pouring out of words
To start you on your way.

You write as though it's easy.
They flow to make it true.
How much loving energy
To write the whole day through.

Poems float free as thistle-down,
Settling where they're found.
Yours root fast like saplings,
Penetrate the ground.

Overpower the reader
Draw him towards the light
Bend him round strange corners
Hidden out of sight.

Let the words be special,
Saying something new.
Cutting out fine patterns,
Seen by only you.

Shaping your own landscape
Seen by only you.

1982

THE SECRETARY'S REVENGE

For Rachel Foster

After six months or little more,
He was no longer held in awe:
Marry a boss and make him pay
I think that he will squirm today.

For dreary years, I typed out letters
For those who thought themselves my betters.
Marry a boss and make him pay
I'm sure that he has squirmed today.

But I'm in charge of him at last,
He'll learn to rue his carefree past.
Marry a boss and make him pay
By God, he really squirmed today.

And now our marriage, like him, grows
Older and wiser in its woes.
I've married a boss and made him pay
He'll go on squirming every day,

Forever, if I have my way.

1984

LOVENOTES

I think I'd comb my hair if I were you,
And what is more, you need a hanky too.
Your shirt is falling out, you're much too fat:
And yet I love you true apart from that.

—

I can't deny
My faults are many,
Unlike my love
Who hasn't any.

1984

THE VIEW FROM MORYN

On the terrace,
Christina stands naked,
beautiful and brown as
– she says – a hazelnut,
looking across the bay
towards the estuary
where yesterday, sunlit,
we stared back at this house
tucked grey and firm
into its private corner,
while no one with no clothes on
looked across at us.

Today, the clouds are low,
the mist wrapped round us
like a sodden towel,
it has been raining forever,
and the view is better
from inside the sitting-room.
Lucky me, to be so privileged;
and poor deprived mariners
and estuary-dwellers,
shielded from the light
by the thickness of Anglesey air.

1985

MIDNIGHT COMFORTS

A Chauvinist's Home Thoughts From Abroad

Not having a gift for languages
Concentrates the insomniac mind wonderfully
On the few shreds of recognizable English
That can usefully be discerned far from home
On a tiny medium-wave receiver.

The Greek is only Greek to me,
And the Turkish, Albanian and Arabic – if that is what
    they are –
Are what they are. Most of the music is impenetrable,
From the mysterious east or worse; while even
    snatches of Mozart
(or Haydn perhaps?) offer no permanent solace or
    connexion.

For I confine my search to words, the BBC World
    Service, no more, no less;
Eureka – a certainty, a sudden burst of news
Unmistakably twelve o'clock high midnight GMT
    British;
And crisp rock-edged Pippa Harben hard on its heels
With the supreme self-indulgence: "News About
    Britain". It glows

With reassurance – David Steel's damages; Thatcher,
    Owen, Gould (who he?)
Each generally electing to accuse the others of low
    treasons,

Multiple betrayal by selling us down every conceivable
    river

Defence-wise, nuclear-foolish; who cares ? It's home !

Until the signal unaccountably inexorably fades and
    fails.

And all one can find to retune to is a Soviet-coloured

Commentary on Fiji, a red-American-read Moscow
    news, and then

"Our man" in Kabul, Boris – God help us –

Filing in Russian, with an almost instant translation
    into

Lancastrian Marxist English. Not exactly what I
    wanted.

If you are reading me now, British Government to
    come

Of whatever hues or parties, then consider this: that
    in exchange for

A small nuclear device, an unimportant surrender of
    sovereignty

(What price South Georgia?), a denial of tax benefits

To millionaires, or rate rebates to the gainfully
    unemployed

(Choose your own most doubtful secondary
    priorities), could you not better

Present us with a certain future

Omnipresent present, an omnipotently potent

Potential signal ? You might just then

Suspect that the distant world could become (Deo
    volente)

A shade better informed (perhaps even wiser and safer)

And certainly better-equipped with the midnight comforts

That I – on Spetsai – and millions far more remote yearn for

From England now (Oh my Bush House, Strand, "This is London" – far away).

Is anyone listening at your end ?

Spetsai, 3 a.m. Greek time, May 1987

NB: This was written just before Mr Brian Gould had fully emerged from his previous antipodean obscurity. By now he has disappeared once more in the general direction of New Zealand. Sic transit...

XAPA – which means 'joy' – is gateway to an almost magical estate, hidden and deserted, at the top of the island of Spetsai. James Foot illustrated it because it was indirectly responsible for our first meeting in 1987.

A PRIVATE JOY

For J

The seasons quicken while the years wear on
And as they pass, the stories stay untold.
It is the price one pays for getting old;
There are no plans, no plots to build upon.

Yet now these unexpected acts of pleasure
Of bodies moving to a single end,
Our newfoundland of love and loving, lend
An old renewed enchantment, throw a measure

Of doubt on time, the past and future fading,
Only the present holds my full attention.
Your sudden beauty moves me to distraction,
My lust's a tonic, an antidote to ageing.

I am, my love, not sad nor overcast
But cherishing these moments while they last.

1987

ANGRY SILENCE

It hangs heavy like a soaked sheet,
feels as clammy as soft dead flesh
– meat on a slab, marriage on the rocks –
and yet is unyielding, inexorable,
like night's middle without a dawn
to follow; there are no ways out.

The anger is not real, but deliberately
contrived, a device to reheat the last
fragments of feeling or to repair a
failing connection; better even to
flail and batter than to yield.
The silence is real enough.

There seems no answer now except for distance.
Tearing the nerves, bewailing and demanding,
begging and pleading, even the sad repetition
of dying songs, words and music, both a
long time gone and not likely to be sung again;
none of these can help – the holes are in the hearts.

May 1987

RICHER AND STRANGER

A Surreyscape

For Ursula Wyndham

Once it was simply a lawn,
neatly kept, sharply defined
and comfortable to live with
in a slightly suburban manner.

Then came a land-change
into something faintly familiar
to those neighbours versed in House
and Garden; the others, prosaically,

watched and wondered, while grottoes grew,
mass-produced statues (from the commercial end
of Venice) arrived, took cover – and peeped
through the carefully-selected bushes.

There were small trees, too, scattered
among cunning flower-beds. It was transmuted,
a miniature eighteenth-century landscape,
lovingly conceived and laid down with joy.

It had become a garden to reckon with.
Such a pity about the house.

1987

NOT TOO LATE FOR LOVING

For Catherine

Early though our days are,
We must treat them true,
Put them to a testing,
Binding me and you.

Finding where our road is,
Going where it leads.
Love has small beginnings
From enchanted seeds.

Pay the tolls we're asked for;
Hand in hand we'll go
On a lovers' journey,
Hoping maps will show

Paths made for our walking
Days for our delight;
Time enough for loving
Holding back the night.

Time enough for loving
Though all journeys end
When the darkness gathers
Round the last blind bend.

Not too late for loving,
The journey's not yet done.
Let us in our testing
Trust the road we're on.

October 1987

A CAMEL TROUVÉ

A profile partly deriving from the Concise Oxford Dictionary

Written 1987

Set by Richard Williams 1997

NB The words in inverted commas form the actual definition of 'camel' that is found in the Concise Oxford Dictionary (Fifth Edition). I wrote the poem in a very approximate camel shape and then waited for ten years until a friend, the distinguished animator Dick Williams (who won an Oscar for 'Who Framed Roger Rabbit?') said while we were playing jazz together, 'I can do that.' And he did!

WAYS

For Catherine

Waiting for you
Seems
The longest way.

—

Lying with you
Feels
The sweetest way.

—

Living with you
Gives
The surest way.

—

Loving with you
Is
The only way.

—

Always.

Putney 1988

UNFINISHED BUSINESS

Aetat 55

This is the way the autumn goes,
The sun is shining and it snows.

Though my friends and colleagues snigger,
I weight-watch with the utmost rigour.

To a Sunday pub where jazz is played,
I've walked a mile for a lemonade.

No food, no wine, what could be worse ?
In sheer frustration, I write verse.

My lady's ill – she feels no better
I stay upstairs, compose a letter.

Letter and verse, not a book review,
Yet that's the one that's overdue.

I envy those whose plans hold steady
While mine prove always not quite ready.

Too old to change, snow's not much fun
I'd best sit quietly in the sun.

But love's relentless, have no doubt;
There's no escape when it's about.

Each time I get my fingers burnt;
There must be tricks I've not yet learnt.

Too late to stop, so once again,
I'll try for joy, and risk the pain.

The sun's still shining while it snows.
For that's the way the autumn goes.

Putney, November 1988

STALEMATE

*For Catherine,
at the Dove, Hammersmith,
Sunday lunch-time*

I thought you joked when after food
You then assumed a sombre mood
And said you'd leave – and take your car –
If I dared smoke a nice cigar.

I did. You upped and dumped me there
To contemplate your vacant chair.
You even sacrificed your pud
By being firm for my own good.

I'd won my battle, lost my war;
You'd made your point but what was more,
An extra punishment you'd give.
A long walk home to where we live.

But then your car came into view.
It still was there – and so were you.
The game was over – and the score ?
We'd fought an honourable draw.

February 1989

THE BIRTH OF TWINS

The first recorded Gemini
Are those you see up in the sky
Order them well; Pollux and Castor
Reversed and rhymed lead to disaster.

One founded Rome; sadly the other
Was terminated by his brother.
And yet now nothing comes between them;
We learn both Romulum and Remum.

A Donne-struck lover, by his troth
Will take so powerful an oath...
Will search for years until he catches
A girl whose metaphysic matches.

Shakespeare made some crafty pluses
From Dromios and Antipholuses.
To novice playwrights, his advice is
That twins are useful stage devices.

Tweedles Dum and Dee fought battles
Re the ownership of rattles.
Inventing such a warlike sample,
Carroll set twins a bad example.

The Bedser boys, Eric and Alec,
Found cricket as a game quite phallic,
With balls and stumps, legs long and fine
And extra slips for bodyline.

What made the young McWhirters set
Their sights on all the mostest yet
That could be culled from near or far
To grace the Guinness Book of R ?

By accident, not from design,
I've missed out all the distaff line,
The Jays, the Bevs, there's Gert and Daisy,
Or were they twins ? My memory's hazy.

But one thing's clear – a double birth
Presages neither grief nor mirth,
Just holds in store for mams and pappies
A double load of dirty nappies.

January 1990

FRIENDS APART

In Memoriam:
Peter King
Jean Jenkins
Jamal Mohammed Ahmed
Bruce Turner

whose books sit on my shelves

The dead are all around me
My joy in them
Turned to ashes and dust
As they are.
Only their books remain
And the nagging memory of
Last letters left unanswered,
Phone calls unmade,
Plans and projects shelved...
All our lives unmade too soon
And all things done and gone
Or left undone and never
To be found again.

Not much wonder then
That as a late and dubious consolation
Heaven might seem to some to house the dead
On perpetual holiday, their last resort.
But not to me; there is no comforting reward.
The only final ending – the painful one
To others – is one's own, as theirs

Are too to those who love them. But
Until that reckoning, I must try
To hold the fading past in focus, still
Remembering, reading, even yearning,
Sifting the ashes, honouring the dust, yet also
Finding and clinging to the living
Who are still around.

January 1991

Although Bruce died after I had written this, I added him to the list. His generous reference to me in 'Hot Air, Cool Music' had put me in the index between Tatum A. and Teagarten J, and such reflected glory deserved to be reciprocated. "Some fun, I'd say, dad !"

RATS

Rats are nasty, rats are vile,
Rats would make a sadist smile,
Clever too and very vicious,
Eat their young – find them delicious.

Black, brown or white, each sick creation
Deserves its loathsome reputation.
Carrying plague and fouling food,
Rats really are extremely crude.

There's not much more to say in fact,
Except that every rat-like act,
With brutish horrid lack of grace,
Reminds rats of the human race.

January 1991

THE LANDLORD COMETH

Not to be born is,
Past all prizing, best.
    Sophocles

Life is a room which gets, alas,
Smaller and darker while years pass.
As for the lease, some excrement
Keeps putting up the bloody rent.
In retrospect, the trick I fear,
Is never to have lodgings here.

June 1991

THE TRUTH ABOUT HOUSEWORK

In the golden far-off Thirties,
Maids toiled for the middle classes.
Only hapless proletarians
Scrubbed their steps and polished brasses.

Then came painful post-war years
When we grew up; we know no others.
No sign yet of women's lib
And most of us relied on mothers.

Later on they rumbled us;
We chaps soon found the chips were down.
Affluence meant household gadgets;
Girls shopped madly round the town.

Laundering clothes and washing dishes
Now are capital-intensive.
Thank the Lord for labour-saving;
Daily helps are so expensive !

Meals are fun from Marks & Spencer,
Drip-dry shirts a benediction.
Though who's to change the throw-away nappies
Can still create domestic friction.

Making beds is no great hassle,
Duvets have transformed our lives.
So the prospects seem quite pleasing
If we choose to leave our wives.

But bachelors gay or straight all must
Learn how to sew and clean and dust.

Port Isaac, June 1991

VERBATIM (con brio)

From a cookery book

"Mozzarella in carrozza",
a popular Italian snack,
is a small sandwich
filled with cheese,
rolled in flour,
dipped in beaten egg,
fried in oil,
and eaten very hot.

January 1992

A POSY OF MIXED METAPHORS

For Richard and Patricia Baker,
Douglas and Jean Airey, Michael Dineen,
Michael and Mary Buckley
Sarah Murray, Ian Simons, Ron Bloomfield

Though love, like gorse, is never out of fashion
It usually leads to anguish, rage and doubt.
And far too many poems, sprung from passion,
Will later wither when the flames go out.

It therefore is a safer proposition
To write a verse to greet some old-found friends.
For friendship offers promise, not contrition,
To celebrate renewal, not an end.

March 1992

A CUSTOMER SERVICE

*For L.M., manager at the
Customer Service Branch,
Bank of Ireland, Slough*

*Come friendly bombs
And fall on Slough.*
John Betjeman

My lovely Louise McEntegart,
I'm not the usual kind of braggart,
But boast a heartfelt need to thank a
Very special personal banker
By telling listeners, all and one,
That Irish banking's much more fun.
For banks, like dentists, are no draw;
I shun them and their works abhor.
It's only when the treatment's finished
I feel relieved, though much diminished.
But now the process is a pleasure,
A trip to Slough's good use of leisure.
My bank account's a joy to see;
Come, friendly Louise, fall on me !

September 1992

ITSQUITEALOGICAL CONCLUSION

Though very fond of life, I would be lying
If I denied that I'm obsessed with dying.
Not as an act of choice but of the heart,
Which once its interest lapses fails to start.
The body's full of signs one can't ignore
Which point relentlessly towards the door.
Will I – or someone else – put out the light ?
And once I'm through it, is it day or night ?
This land of no return and its topology
Are now the focus for my eschatology,
For as these last things loom, what does come after ?
I dread to hear the sound of ghostly laughter,
But equally I fear my days will cease,
To be replaced by everlasting peace.

These gloomy thoughts are giving me neuralgia,
I think I must take refuge in nostalgia.
So while I last, I'll fill these final hours
With girls and jazz and poems and food and flowers.

October 1992

A BELATED NOTE OF CONDOLENCE

For Jeannette in memory of Jacques Kupferman, 1987

I noticed in the Literary Review
A glowing piece about a book by you.*

Your house was lit; I knocked upon the door
To find your daughter sitting on the floor.

I borrowed Mina's copy – signed by Mum –
Read in an hour enough to strike me dumb,

To make me know you as I never have,
To glimpse your grief, regret my lack of love,

Admire the slow and lucid growth of hope,
And through it showing others how to cope.

A truthful tender book which, when I'd finished,
Left me much moved but curiously diminished.

I wish I'd realized your pain and heeded it,
And offered comfort when you really needed it.

Port Isaac, 1992

* *When the Crying's Done, A journey through widowhood.*
Jeannette Kupferman

GLADYS, HILDA AND ALL THESE

A warning to intending parents

Mrs Wilson, Mrs Thatcher
(Mary and Margaret to their friends?)
Rightly shunned their other forenames,
Left them to the satirists' pens.

Where are they now, the Gwens and Madges,
Ethel (William's sister) Brown ?
Ada, Percy, Jabez, Cuthbert,
Silas and Seth have all left town.

Names of uncles, aunts and cousins
Are expunged from current use,
Soon to be joined by burnt-out favourites,
Darren , Sharon, Tracey, Bruce.

Some make unexpected comebacks,
Sophie, Emily, Sam and Ben.
Even Marmaduke and Cecil
Pop up every now and then.

But single names are always risky,
Role models change, and fashions cease.
So leave room for evasive action
From Gladys, Hilda and all these.

December 1992

I AND YOU KNOW

A defeated Scrabble player's key to the
divine plan concerning Brazilian mammals

For James Foot and Margaret Last, enthusiasts both

Not many – not I –
only Scrabble devotees
can distinguish an ai
from a unau with ease.

Now an ai has three toes;
so what's common to both ?
Ais and two-digit unaus
are twin species of sloth.

From such clues, I deduce
that God's bias is absurd
(lets you use up your u's;
makes a two-letter word).

He invents Evolution
to worldwide acclaim,
then in verbal collusion
helps you win that damned game.

Port Isaac, April 1993

BACHELOR HABITS AT SIXTY

But for me, the house is empty,
Children, wives and lovers gone.
No more talk and family fun;
Living by myself is plenty.

At an age when compromises
Have become too hard to bear,
My books and pictures, desk and chair,
All lead me to my own devices.

If my bed at night is lonely,
Daytimes leave me space to choose:
Music, silence, sloth and booze;
Marriage is for heroes only.

Port Isaac, April 1993

Piano Recital by
David Nawarauckas.

Mozart - Sonata C major. K 545
Beethoven - Sonata C minor, op 13
'Pathetique'

Schubert - Impromptus:
    opus 142 (posthumous) No. 2 Ab major
    opus 90 Eb major

Chopin - 3 Waltzes:
    opus 18 Eb major
    opus 64 No.1 Db major
    opus 64 No.2 C# minor
    Fantasia Impromptu opus 66

Berceuse Db major OP 57

Saturday, 1st March 2003
Putney

Piano Recital by
David Nawarauckas.

Mozart - Sonata C major. K 545
Beethoven - Sonata C minor, op 13
'Pathetique'

Shubert - Impromptus:
    opus 142 (posthumous) No. 2 Ab major
    opus 90 Eb major

Chopin - 3 Waltzes:
    opus 18 Eb major
    opus 64 No.1 Db major
    opus 64 No.2 C# minor.
    Fantasia Impromptu opus 66
Berceuse Db major op 57

Saturday, 1st March 2003
Putney

Piano Recital by
David Nawarauckas.

Mozart - Sonata C major. K545
Beethoven - Sonata C minor op 13
'Pathétique'

Shubert - Impromptus:
    opus 142 (posthumous) No. 2 Ab major
    opus 90 Eb major

Chopin - 3 Watzes:
    opus 18 Eb major
    opus 64 No.1 Db major
    opus 64 No.2 C# minor.
    Fantasia Impromptu opus 66
Bercease Db major OP 57

Saturday, 1st March 2003
Putney.

Piano Recital by
David Nawarauckas.

Mozart - Sonata C major. K545
Beethoven - Sonata C minor op 13
        'Pathetique'

Shubert - Impromptus:
        opus 142 (posthumous) No. 2 Ab major
        opus 90 Eb major

Chopin - 3 Waltzes:
        opus 18 Eb major
        opus 64 No.1 Db major
        opus 64 No.2 C# minor
        Fantasia Impromptu opus 66
    Berceuse Db major OP 57

Saturday, 1st March 2003
        Putney

Piano Recital by
David Nawarauckas.

Mozart - Sonata C major. K 545
Beethoven - Sonata C minor op 13
'Pathetique'

Shubert - Impromptus:
opus 142 (posthumous) No. 2 Ab major
opus 90 Eb major

Chopin - 3 Waltzes:
opus 18 Eb major
opus 64 No 1 Db major
opus 64 No 2 C# minor.
Fantasia Impromptu opus 66

Berceuse Db major OP 57

Saturday 1st March 2003
Putney

PRICKLY HEAT

For AA

So far from home I've never been before,
So far and yet this Indian Ocean town
Has curious echoes which unlock the past,

Amongst the temples, mosques and Hindu gods,
Red-brick Victorian buildings, dated slang,
And boys playing cricket down on Galle Face Green.

The Portuguese and Dutch left traces too,
Fonsecas and Pereiras, and the burghers;
And tea, the best and worst I've ever drunk.

The climate of a gentle English spring,
But that's the air-conditioning. Outside,
The central heating's turned up much too high.

A warm and friendly people, yet beneath,
An underlying abyss lies there unseen,
Buddhist and Tamil violence in the blood –

Or in the heat. The ordinary folk
Abhor the killings, doubt the politicians;
But – just like Ireland – loyalties abide.

The educated rich live well; the poor
Share no enlightened future, see no hope,
The beggars, cripples, children on the game.

But Brits and Aussies reinforce their lives
(which Anglicized Sri Lankans seem to share)
In close approximations to a pub.

This Sunday after drunken jazz, I spent
A monsoon-sodden evening contemplating
The swings between the runs and constipation.

The monks in saffron robes, the bullock carts,
The kids with cobras, one stray elephant,
It's not like home, but still all too familiar

From childhood books, Kim's India sanitized.
It's Serendip, but not quite paradise.
And yet I have reluctantly to say
I am entranced for much of every day.

Colombo, Sri Lanka, May 1993

A RETIRED OLD GENTLEMAN
IS DIPLOMATICALLY REBUFFED
AT THE HIGHEST LEVEL

In hope of lunch – or even dinner –
I signed the High Commissioner's book.
I even left my card so he'd
Reciprocate next time he'd look.

Only Elizabeth (with Philip)
Once had a page all to herself.
Now no one signs; a frosty silence
Has left me firmly on the shelf.

My social climbing days are over;
Not even as a consolation,
A splendid crested billet-doux,
A Royal Birthday invitation !

The times have changed *et nos in illis;*
Those ancient courtesies are old-hat.
Next time, I'll set my sights much lower,
The British Consul's where I'm at.

Colombo, Sri Lanka, June 1993

TAKE GREAT CARE IN THE HILLS

Da Silva's splendid Book of Lankan Snakes
says kraits and cobras always are in season,
and found in beds and kitchens. That's the reason
I'm going to spend the night locked in the jakes.

Kandy, Sri Lanka, June 1993

THE LOTUS FROM KANDY

Up in the not-so-high but blissful
cool green hills lies an ancient
lakeside capital, with a rich royal past,
a crowded present and a tourist trade
sharply focused on a holy relic, a tooth
of the Lord Buddha.

In his cream and golden temple, prayers
are made to him, flowers brought for him, and his
teachings still echo after the blossoms die
(as indeed so shall we all). *Do away
with all desires, and find truth and goodness
within yourself* –

Then the Diyawadana Nilame, temple guardian
and custodian of the tooth, gave me a lotus.
*It grows on dark and impenetrable waters, and yet
remains both pure and beautiful* – perhaps
somewhere in the heart of that matter is the heart
of all that matters.

Kandy, Sri Lanka, June 1993

ACCIDENTAL DEATHS

It's easy to forget that death lurks near
just out of sight of every driver's view.
The car's a deadly weapon but so few
of those who use them show a proper fear.
It's only when a sudden fatal lapse
of judgement leads on to a final kill
and when the ruined body's lying still
not one but two entangled lives collapse,
the dead beyond recall, but for the living,
the overdriven mind can't hold; at last,
what hid the future, now repeats the past.
There's no quick way to find your own forgiving;
and every living dawn, as you are waking,
inexorably, you're sweating, scared and shaking.

Colombo, June 1993

LIFELINES

At sixty, it's patently obvious
Life isn't a long-lasting flame.
The trouble with life is when you find out
It's a limited-over game.

And you, and all those playing with you
(Once you know that you're on the same side)
Are only just starting to get the hang
When the pitch starts to move and you slide,

With no strength in yourself to support you
As you lean on the ones that you choose;
There isn't much else for your balance
And without them, you'll probably lose

Those last fleeting moments of pleasure
At a time when you need others more.
So hang onto your friends and your lovers
As you stumble along towards the door.

Colombo, Sri Lanka, 1993

STATISTICAL ADVICE TO EXPATRIATES

(The largest number of deaths of those living overseas come
from heart attacks, drowning and motor accidents.)

Abroad is fun,
What joy it triggers,
Until you read
These frightening figures

Which seem to show
Without much fuss
That all you do
Is dangerous.

Don't work, you'll crack,
Don't swim, you'll drown.
And cars, for sure,
Will let you down.

But if you'd rather
Not be dead,
Then stay at home;
Don't leave your bed.

Or take a chance
That you'll survive;
Be wild, enjoy
And stay alive.

Till you run into
AIDS or cancer,
Your goose is cooked
There is no answer.

So better not
To know such horror.
Don't read today;
You'll ruin tomorrow.

Sri Lanka, 1993

GONE:

In memoriam John Wain, 24 May 1994

When he went over, without much warning,
To whatever lies across that final border,
For a few days he was more with me
In memory and dreams than ever before.
Then I came back; I needed once again
To read his poems, live within his novels
And share his favourite music, Fats and Louis.

Most of all, I remembered – as did all who
    cherished him –
The wit, the fun, the kindliness,
The joy he gave – a learned loving friend –
A generous spirit preserving to the very last
A zest for pubs and country walks,
And a proper appreciation of pretty girls.

Requiescat in luce.

May 1994

WALKING ON THE SPOT

Had I the strength to put my life in order,
To sort out all the rubbish, pay the bills,
Discard the useless debris of the past
Kept only for sentimental reasons,

Even so, I know too well that faced
With a clean sheet, a tidy desk,
All debts and doubts settled, every pathway open
And not a single hostage to fortune,

Within a week or so, I'd find myself
Back in the old chaos, hanging on for dear life
To fragments long accumulated, the present
    propped up
By last year's letters,

Papers and problems piling, all roads closed.
This, it seems, is where I started.
So why not accept inertia, conserve energy,
Practise passive survival as a living art.

August 1994

LIFETIME COP-OUT

I never consciously confront;
Why can't I let my anger out,
Not hide it like a Swiss account ?

My gut reactions don't get through;
Am I too scared to scream and shout,
To rant and rave as others do ?

No use erupting when I'm harassed,
Why should I let my anger out ?
The words sing dumb; I'm too embarrassed.

Avoidance is the path I've followed.
Too well-controlled to scream and shout,
My secret bile is better swallowed.

So if I'm bruised by what I'm feeling,
Rage might provide a kind of healing.
But much too scared to scream and shout,
I still can't let my anger out.

September 1994

BACK TO BASICS

"There is a last, even of last times."
Samuel Beckett

"Now see I that warmth's the very stuff of poesy."
T. E. Hulme

Always, often, sometimes, never;
Each lies heavy on my heart.
Looking back can't last forever,
Ending, slowing, running, start.

Searching, finding, loving, losing,
Why am I so out of breath ?
Last of last times not my choosing,
Birth and youth, decline and death.

Hot and warm and cold and freezing,
Too old for love, too late to care;
Best turn on the central heating;
Fire and water, earth and air.

October 1994

SEIZE THE LIVING MOMENTS

For Russell Grant

Such time that's left seems too compressed.
Living by day, to write at night ?
A lonely trade; one gets depressed.

I doubt my energies will last.
There's not much time to put things right.
The leaves are falling far too fast.

I don't intend to start again.
My shortening days need sleep at night,
To stay awake is too much pain.

The rhymes dry up; the feeling's gone;
I can't find time, the words aren't right,
And yet there's business not yet done.

So as day fades, look to the night,
There's still time left to get it right.

March-April 1995

FLYING BLIND

After Robert Graves

The Pipistrelle or Common Bat
Cares not nor wonders where it's at
When flying blind to make a kill
By bio-electronic skill.

It navigates the darkest air
And, squeaking, swoops; it has the flair
Of using ultra-sonic sound,
Avoiding trees, skimming the ground,

To grab its supper in full flight,
The flies and beetles of the night.
Such carnivores must scare the hell
Out of their prey – and me as well !

April 1995

DORA ADELAIDE HARVEY RAEBURN,
born 17 June 1906

DORA'S AMAZING!
~ caring, kind and clever;
At ninety now
    she's as involved as ever.
Her mind's still bright
    nor do the years confound her ~
Remarkable how the world
    lights up around her.

June 1996

TOO POOR TO OWN COWS

(Spectator competition entry [O's only])

No job, no dosh,
Not wont to cosh.
Oh God, oh sorrow,
No food tomorrow !

April 1996

D.I.Y.

On a
Normal day
Any
Number
Is
Suitable
To play
Singly

June 1996

TOGETHER

Feeling an
Urgent need for
Carnal
Knowledge
Is
Naturally selective
Group behaviour.

June 1996

RUMBLINGS

For Daryl, Patricia and Atticus

In this plastic pedestrian precinct, bursting with
   noise,
I wander towards the epicentre of violent sound,
music drowning voices,
where clusters of beautiful boys and girls,
black-haired, long-legged and ready
– though not perhaps as ready as they think –
sprawl, brooding, in the ear-splitting cafés
of their lives.

They are the future in waiting,
certain in their lack of years and grace,
ignoring the other older world
which in turn reciprocates,
allowing their Ptolomaïdan youthquakes
to subside without notice.

From less vulnerable observation posts,
wizened, black-clad grandmothers gather,
brown, wrinkled veterans regroup,
each gender carefully keeping its own company,
all survivors of their own sex wars
of fifty years ago

– They will learn just as we learned;
and all things pass as we are passing –

Back at the mating grounds of the young,
saturate with songs and sexual promise,
even the world-hardened ancient gods might
prefer to walk the long way round
and avoid the din.

Ptolomaïda, Greece, May 1996

THOUGHTS ON A SPANISH TERRACE

For Claudia Burgoyne

This is the last of Europe, so close
to Africa that the Pillars of Hercules,
Gibraltar, Ceuta and the Riff
make up the distant backcloth.

Britain, says Radio Four – far off and faint –
is cold and bleak and very wet.
Here even the low-angled sun
has winter warmth in its Mediterranean way.

We sit on the slope of a great backed bowl,
green in parts but rimmed around
by bare rocky hills. There are few, very few, people,
little clusters in newly (annually, by diktat)
white-painted villages. Under such modern façades,
their Moorish past is not quite hidden;
its roots and centre hold, hard and dangerous.

It is startlingly peaceful, easy to forget
the nuns tipped over the precipice in nearby Ronda,
eyes gouged out with teaspoons, airborne murder and
    landlocked rape,
and, in an earlier age, my forefathers expelled
in 1492 (odd how an American door opened
when Spanish gates closed).

For these are the lands of my ancient Jewish past;
behind me Toledo, across the water Tangier and Meknes.
and then beyond them Sfax and Tripoli,
Malta, Livorno and all parts eastward
with my Gibraltarian kinsmen almost in touching distance
(but who wants to touch kinsmen?)

Across this network of ancestral places,
my many great grandparents, rabbis and merchants,
– some prosperous, exhibiting public recognition in vice-
     consular ease;
but mostly, I suspect, crammed into urban Arab ghettos –
criss-crossed the sea to trade and, incidentally,
to find wives and husbands, seek advancement
and,suitcases packed anticipating pogroms or plague,
to escape if still alive.

History and landscape then, both harsh and anxious;
but in the here-and-now, in these upmarket hills
where cowbells, crickets and passing horsemen's voices
provide the only mild intrusion, this house – each house –
has comfort and space, privacy, dogs and horses,
six acres of land and views to kill for.
For tea- and rubber-planters, Kenyan farmers and
     colonial DCs,
Spain is the second coming, an expatriate's Nirvana.

But staying here is not to feel at home
despite the hot sun, the cheap brandy, bull rings,
and breakfasts under an orange tree.

To feel at home in time and country is nurture
and conditioning. These warm delights are temporary;
my own strong sense of place is not my ancestors'.
I am a temperate old man, sentimental and nostalgic
– I'd miss the winters too.

And so, eschewing wolves and bears, snakes and sharks,
I must go back to where my ladder starts
(not Yeats but Brooke and Browning), back to England,
London and Cornwall, avoiding if I can
most aspects of the brand-new year to come,
having no truck with any definitions of PC,
nor all the new horrors acronymically presented
as RSI, ME, MS and AIDS.

In what time's left, I'll choose my version of the present,
play geriatric tennis, and antique classic jazz,
revisit old movies, books and paintings
and reject the whole of rock and pop, style gurus and
    Turner prizes.
As for politics and religion, I'll leave my prejudices
    untouched,
take my pleasures from the things I understand.

The trick is not to manage change
but to evade it. I think – for a little while – I can.
Meanwhile, I'll sit on this terrace in the sun
and enjoy the view.

Gaucin, Spain, December 1996
Port Isaac, January 1997

1996

Another year gone, it's the end of December;
seems just like the others, though I can't quite remember.

The government's finished; the royals make me sick;
the England supporters are pining for Hick.

In Ireland and Israel, the mix as before,
they're hoping for peace and preparing for war.

As for Europe and EMU, I'd rather not know
how the chaps who're in charge plan to finish the show.

The best lack conviction, the worst are intense.
I can't tell the difference – I'll sit on the fence.

I'm not going bankrupt; I'm not getting wealthy.
I'm looking my age while not feeling unhealthy.

Except for my appetite, nothing's to blame
that I can't see my toes, but I'm fat just the same.

Despite diabetes and blood-pressure pills,
it might take a few years before one of them kills.

The usual old Christmas cards, bar one or two;
some old friends have gone, though not yet me or you.

The rain goes on raining, the snow falls more thickly.
Another year's starting – they pass far too quickly.

Port Isaac, 1 January 1997

DID I REALLY MEAN THAT ?

Beauty is truth but is Truth beauty ? No,
not by a long chalk, my dad would have said.
The craft of verse, to shape words to be read
as things of beauty often spoils the flow
and balance of ideas which come and go,
shifting and splintering till you've lost the thread.

When asked exactly what you meant, evade
the old romantics' clichés; now you know
that words you wrote last night no longer ring
out truthful in the cold mean light of day.
The truth is that the Truth got in the way
when what you wanted was to make words sing.

Beauty's all right if you let loose a singer on it;
but most truth's far too hard to put your finger on it.

Port Isaac, January 1997

SOME POETS DIED TOO YOUNG TO VENTURE THOUGHTS ON LATER-LIFE ADVENTURE

Yet I love thee without art,
Ancient person of my heart.

Lord Rochester (1647-1680)

So would you go no more a-roving,
let warmth and safety rule your life ?
Looking your last on all things lovely,
are you contented with your wife ?

Rage, if you like, against the dying
of the light, but yet remember
many good things still can happen
before the end of your December.

So rove on from time to time,
looking for ladies more mature.
You're not too old to court surprises
though the chances may get fewer.

You needn't break the bloody glass;
what's lost of youth is gained in cunning.
Don't give up; with any luck,
some pretty girl may soon come running

Towards a source of cash and comfort,
wisdom too; she'll surely settle
for a lunch-time's secret pleasures
which should keep you in fine fettle.

Time to learn that youthful anguish
is much less fun than grown-up joys.
The moment's come for you to be now
among the men not with the boys.

As good in autumn as in spring,
a double life is just the thing.

Kentish Town, February 1997

OLD TIMERS' BLUES:

For all the Crouch End All-Stars past and present
"Oh play that thing !"
[traditional refrain in "Dippermouth Blues"]

The days are passing; not much to report.
Retired old gents have little to report.
No doubt about it; time is getting short.

Waiting with patience for our next band blow,
But pubs are hard to find; no place to blow.
And times are harder; no one wants to know.

The greats are history – they've gone on their way;
They're still our heroes, theirs is still the way.
But time's against us; it allows no stay.

We watch each other; though no one makes a fuss.
With age and drink, who needs to make a fuss ?
There's no disputing, time hangs over us.

We're not in touch with any current crap,
Rock, pop, and rap – to jazzers, it's all crap.
Leave that for kids, it's time's own tourist trap.

Max Jones once said, "Jazz music's underground."
That's where we'll all be soon, down underground;
But time's a-wasting – let's go make that sound.

And as we play, I hope we've got it wrong,
That boys and girls unborn won't think it wrong
In times to come, to play our kind of song.

Port Isaac, 1997

MY ENTIRE HAIKU
COLLECTION AT LEAST AT THIS
MOMENT IN MY LIFE

LAST MARTIAN GASPS

[A haiku on the discovery in
Antarctica of an ancient
meteorite containing traces of
possible bacterial life on Mars
long before there was life on
earth.   New Statesman,
August 1996, competition
winner]

No hope of lifelines
nor yet earthly sympathy,
only post-mortems.

August 1996

LONG-DISTANCE HAIKU

Maharajah rides
his elephant up a hill
trumpeting trunk calls.

January 1997

RED OR BROWN HAIKU

Not exactly an
easy decision to take
when the chips are down.

July 1997

THANKS GLOTTALLY-STOPPED
AND NASALLY-CHALLENGED MAKE
A DOUBLE HAIKU

Speech impediments
and colds cause the same problems;
haiku very much.

July 1997

MY LAST HAIKU

Enough of this crap;
Such a mannered verse format
No longer thrills me

July 1997

But......

NOT SO EASY, LIVING GREEN

For Daryl and Patricia

Carless in Crete,
they walk a tiring road.
setting their faces against
the comfortable choices,
   the instant answers.

There are no bibles or maps;
they write their own, draw
home-made plans, navigate
untested routes into
   an unknown future.

Caring, fighting, and clinging,
holding to their small needs
in an indifferent world,
theirs is the heart of love
   in action.

Hania, October 1997
London, November 1997

A TRUE EUROPEAN

For A. T. at two-and-a-half.

Little Atticus, my grandson,
fluffy, blond and fluent in Greek,
will he ever lay his hands on
Shakespeare, cricket, Pick of the Week ?

Playing with Cretan kids, he knows
he's one of them – and so do they.
Will his little grieving show
when his time comes to go away ?

Two years more and then to Spain,
a pick-and-mix life he'll have had.
Will ye no come back again,
My English, Jewish, wee Scots lad ?

Hania, Crete, Greece, October 1997
Port Isaac, November 1997

TWO BLEAK FACES

Look back, look forward – but where am I now ?
And have I any choice in where I'm going ?
The world is full of pitfalls, nothing showing,
all just around the corner. I'll allow
that horoscopes and dreams claim to provide
the best and worst that life can hold in store.
All lies; reality petrifies me more.
From God and art, no solace and no guide,
and as for people, devious, sly and dumb.
I try to please – but when I turn within,
my dark and secret nightmares soon begin:
I somehow know the terror's yet to come.

I smile and smile, the only thing to do –
while wondering, is it the same for you ?

November 1997

A DOOR OF ONE'S OWN

For Tom Stacey

From a once-shared house,
this is a quiet public statement
about a new life – starting again.

The rite of safe proprietary passage
unencumbered by furniture and paintings
echoing the past is a mirror to independence.

It has a ring of truth about it
now making, after so many years,
not a call to war but a peace declaration.

This move towards an armistice
grants the ultimate civil liberty
behind a separate entrance.

Kentish Town, January 1998

FORTY YEARS ON

For Nicol Williamson

My memory fades fast;
yours seems to survive,
a powerful motor
for keeping alive

lost people and voices
that glittered and shone,
the enchantments of youth.
Now ambition's long gone;

bodies bending and breaking
and minds at half-mast,
it's a dangerous hobby
resurrecting the past.

Yet each scene's an epiphany
which I cherish because
you know better than I do
the young man I was.

November 1997

MUCH LATER ON

After a happy evening with
Sarah Ereira, Alan Ereira, Elizabeth Smith,
Douglas Hill and Catherine Raeburn

"...the forgetfulness and the solipsism
that enable the rest of us to bluff our
way towards happiness.".

Lucy Hughes-Hallett, in a review

When skating on thin ice,
our safety is our speed.

Ralph Waldo Emerson

In the small dark hours, when no one else can
touch upon my innermost life,
I'm forced to think of what I am;
no help from children, friends or wife.

I'm on my own, no players to bluff;
drink and such comforts can't intrude.
Am I quite happy ? All that stuff
now seems so pointless, otiose, crude.

Forgetful ? Yes, the greater part
of pain and anger's best forgotten;
to be thick-skinned's a useful art
to practise when one's feeling rotten.

While as for being solipsistic,
I do like living inside myself.
I'm not by nature pessimistic
so joy still flickers if my health

allows me – so far – to ignore
the symptoms of my own decline.
I'd skate much faster round the floor
if God's old skating rink were mine.

So temporize; lay off all bets;
stifle that self-revealing view.
However dark your own life gets,
the one you've got to bluff is you.

Kentish Town, June/July 1998

REJECTION AND AFTER

For D.T. and all of us

Why do most horses not win races ?
Some can't; some do.
Too much seed spilt in darkened places ?
The hits are few.
"Why won't they read the stuff I write ?"
There's no debt owing.
How do they choose those in the light ?
Somehow, they're glowing.

More self-exposure, pain, depression ?
All shame's now gone.
So what chance now for self-expression ?
Writer, write on !

Hania, Crete, June 1998

DOWN BUT NOT OUT

"The best lack all conviction,
while the worst are full of passionate intensity."

W. B. Yeats

The joys of passionate intensity were never quite my kind
    of game;
to be lacking all conviction seemed an easier way to be,
more comfortably painless, less disturbing in the frame,
not releasing hidden demons we were never meant to see.

Then why, I sometimes wonder, in my dark unloving act,
are the images I conjure up so vicious, cruel, distasteful ?
My mind's half-hidden messages seem to work quite well
    in fact
but the part of me which summons them feels guilty,
    mean and hateful.

These sweaty conscious nightmares have no place in my
    reality
(although they help me understand some violent horrors
    of the past).
I package them and store them, thoughts of unrelieved
    banality,
and use them as a last resort when lust no longer lasts.

For age and failing powers mean that the fun of love's
 departed.
Clapped-out old male machinery's driven by brimstone at
 the least;
no passion, no intensity, just blind conviction that the
 heart has
given up on its loving; all that's surviving is the beast.

Sex in every form is fading; can one learn to live without it ?
Chance encounters – unaccountably – are becoming
 very few.
But heaven too has aphrodisiacs. When it happens, let's
 all shout it
from the rooftops that a brand-new girl has broken into view.

There's nothing like a surge of love to resurrect lost
 potency,
to excise demons so they're only seen and heard in hell.
To hell too with lost conviction and with passionate
 intensity;
let your living and your loving be enough to keep you well.

Let your living and your loving be enough to keep you
 well.

Hania, Crete, June 1998

A SERENDIPITOUS NIGHT WITH CALLIOPE,
A GIRL NOT MENTIONED IN THE GUIDE BOOKS

Not just a muse of epic fire
who poets hope will still inspire
but also a XANIA taverna
where one's friends could quickly learn a
lot about superior, cheap Greek cooking.
At the Med-side, one's protected
by transparent screens, erected
to keep the wind and waves at bay
while we enjoy the end of day,
to warm our sunset all the time we're looking.

Lots of Cretans, not one tourist
(except me), this is the surest
way to find some proper peace,
an enclave of traditional Greece,
gorging on souvlaki and kalamarakia,
retsina, beer and araki,
down beside the wine-dark sea.
Girl at next-door table's pissed;
none the worse for that, she's kissed
my grandson. It all makes the evening sparkier.

Calliope, queen of all the muses,
no one sensible refuses
too much to drink, a lot to eat,
a chance to sit there at your feet,
escaping from the tripper-sodden beaches.

123

A little on-the-spot research
– leave all your guide books in the lurch –
and trust your judgement to discover
a classier joint than any other;
that's just the lesson serendipity teaches !

Hania/XANIA, Crete, June 1998

A PARIAH HOWLS

*In politically-incorrect memory of Charles Stuart Calverley
(Ode to Tobacco) and Mr Bacon of Cambridge, the
tobacconist (now only marked by a memorial tablet in a
boutique)*

"I'll be revenged on the whole pack of you."
Malvolio in *Twelfth Night*

Do dinner hosts and guests inside
feel *Schadenfreude* which they hide
when – smoking – I am thrust outside ?

Like Cnut, I cannot turn the tide
while that old weakness they deride;
from my own house, I'm cast outside !

Both cold and wet, I raged and cried.
No use; as in formaldehyde,
her heart is set. I stay outside.

For twenty years and more I tried
to tell myself I'd stopped. I lied.
Perhaps I'm better off outside.

But this dog's day can't be denied,
and now I know the time's arrived,
I'll throw the whole foul pack outside !

Port Isaac, July 1998

FAG ENDS

For John Cox who understands.

But when my hate-poem's theme I ponder,
I realize "pack"s a *double-entendre.*
This Freudian slip's no accident;
It's clear exactly what it meant.
As ten a day might lead to sorrow,
I'll give up cigarettes tomorrow
With joy. Though if I fail, instead,
I'll hide a pack under my bed !

Port Isaac, July 1998 (next day)

NB: The writer has not smoked since.

NATURAL CAUSES

Boucher, the French painter, disliked
Nature as being "too green and badly lit".

Battle-green for danger,
darkening green for gloom,
fading green for sickness,
churchyard green for doom.

Ill-lit in a coffin,
ill-lit at a wake;
ill-lit for the last
six feet he'll ever take.

Buxom girls' pink bottoms,
glowing in courtly light;
maidens, shepherds, cupids,
Boucher got his options right.

But having done, he entered
the realm he'd long foreseen,
reductio ad absurdum,
badly-lit – and green.

Port Isaac, July 1998

HOW ODD TO BE A PYLON

For Dr Jane Sackville-West

As I struggle to the bath at seven-thirty,
piped and wired to a trolley, I get shirty.
My daily ablutions
reach no quick solutions,
I'd be far better off staying dirty.

Cardiac Intensive Care Unit,
University College Hospital, London
10 September 1998

A FORTIETH ANNIVERSARY JINGLE

For Caryle Steen, formerly my G.P.,
and her psychiatrist husband Bernard Adams,
on the occasion of their ruby wedding celebration

Once I did what Caryle ordered;
she kept my health up to the mark.
But now we're equal partners
playing ball games in the park.

Bernard is a "mind" chap,
no bodies at any price;
though when I really had a pain,
he gave the right advice.*

This new and loving friendship
is for me a rare delight;
they're worth their weight in rubies
so this clearly is their night.

We wish them joy and health and fun,
and (one more hope to speak)
that we can go on playing tennis
at our geriatric peak.

* *"Go and see your proper doctor immediately. You may have*
had a heart attack." (He had had one himself, on a tennis court!)
I went, I was hospitalized (see 'How odd to be a pylon') reified,
operated on in a small way (angiogram); I hadn't. Indigestion !

Kentish Town 28 September 1998

EPITHALAMION

For the Walkers

Now all is done, bring home the bride againe.
Edmund Spenser

Dear Daniel and sweet Marianne,
you've tied the knot so no one can
deny your rights now to explore
your bed, your house, the park next door.

to study birds and bees and flowers,
so taking up the daylight hours
that then, self-taught, as man and wife
you'll need from us no facts of life;

except it won't be long until
your heirs arrive. You'll get your fill
of dirty nappies, sleepless nights,
you'll feel like death and look real frights.

The small get large with undue haste,
make friends, have parties, get a taste
for clothes to put them on the map
(you'll shop at Oxfam, they at Gap!).

Then fags and joints, their grown-up heaven,
not good when only just eleven;
and not much later, romance blooms.
Heart-racked, they're moping in their rooms.

When real sex comes, the question's still
"Should we now put her on the pill?"
and warn – apart from having babies –
of horrid lurgies, worse than rabies.

But after years of sweat and pain
your lives and house are yours again.
The cares of parenthood you're shedding
(until you pay for each child's wedding).

So make the most of this bright spring.
The best's to come; of joy we sing
and love. Though when your mums start knitting,
get them lined up for baby-sitting.

9 October 1998, Kentish Town

The private reader may borrow, modify or shorten this wedding poem as appropriate. For example, the first line could read:

"Delightful lady, nice young man…"

Greetings-card manufacturers, on the other hand, are welcome to negotiate with the writer.

TIME AND TASTE

An intonation for ancients

Arthur Ransome, Ronald Frankau,
  Round the Horne, Flanders and Swann,
Grable, Flynn, the Saint, Tom Lehrer,
  Like steam on G.W.R., long gone.

Brahms and Simon, Arrau, Priestley,
  Louis Armstrong, Compton, May,
Punch, the Listener, and Encounter
  All seem very far away.

Contrariwise, pères Waugh and Amis,
  Auden, Blyton, Beatrix Potter,
Dumbo, Pooh, and Toad still flourish –
  And river care's restored the otter.

The undead live – like Aleister Crowley –
  There's A. Cooke, Pet and A.C. Clark(e),
Weekend steam-trains, monthly Oldies,
  Come out to play, it's not yet dark!

Port Isaac, 1998

NB Tom Lehrer is actually alive and well and teaching mathematics. He gave up satire many years ago because the real world seemed too satirical to be parodied!

Punch and GWR bear no relation to their contemporary equivalents.

Readers might like to chant their own lists, perhaps to the tune of 'Frère Jacques' (which doesn't fit these verses).

WAITING FOR WINTER:
PORT ISAAC IN NOVEMBER

Most fishing's finished,
The visitors gone,
It seems an age
Since the sun last shone.

Too bleak and damp
  to sit and walk,
But a perfect day
For old-times talk.

1998

THESE WILL SURELY DO

For my grandchildren
Laura, Jethro, Atticus, Erik and Pearl

This is a song for you;
There'll be days of magic, light and sound,
Excitement, pleasures, joys new-found,
A world with loving friends around.
As a start, that will probably do.

This is a wish for you;
Follow your talents, hone your skills,
And find true passions; boredom kills.
But earn enough to pay your bills;
On the whole, that will certainly do.

This is a prayer for you;
May you stay safe from every storm,
Let strength and calm be your life's norm,
Be brave, cool, happy – and keep warm!
With some luck, that might just about do.

Port Isaac / on a GWR train / Putney 1998

CHEESE DREAMS

*For Angelica Jacob, who wrote in her novel
"Fermentation": "my dreams ...were very vivid,
like short films with a story to tell. "*

You've set your lady in a cunning weave
of cheese, the unborn growing, by love deceived,
and sex in strange excesses. She discovers
new joys and fears when overheated lovers

burn on each boiling day. She's thrust apart
to the secret private places of the heart
and groin, digs deep in mythic sexual urging.
But why are cheese and pregnant life converging?

Should I, a lusting voyeur, have the right
to deconstruct her story, aim my sights
so close to home when love and lovers fail?
Not mine to judge – let cheeses tell the tales.

Her child is born so one last human cheese
spurs on Annunciatory wit – to please
Our Lady with angelic impregnation,
while still your lady waits; that's "Fermentation"!

Port Isaac April 1999

A LAUREATE FOR ALL SEASONS

"Candidates," remarked Sunday,
"are only required to answer
eight of the seventeen questions…"
"The Man Who Was Thursday", G.K. Chesterton.

By the time this reaches print, short of disaster
the contest will be over; he or she
who's been selected by the powers-that-be
will be quaffing butts of sack. This poetaster

(only a rhyme, no value judgement falling
on Motion, Duffy, Abse, still all running,
or other hidden contenders, they're the cunning
practitioners of a high and noble calling.)

will be on course to honour – or make you sick –
each royal occasion, wedding, birth or death
in joy or sorrow. But don't hold your breath;
the output might be less than Royal Musick.

Enough of this, it's rather hard
to write this kind of rhyming quatrain.
I'm glad I'm not an aspirant bard;
it really gives one head and heart pain.

Let's try and put it in perspective,
Austin and Bridges no more please,
a long time gone – the new invective
would blow the royals from the trees.

But most prefer tradition; they'd draw a curtain
on Harrison, Walcott, Heaney, left-wing asses,
Another Masefield or J.B.'d be certain
to please the crowds, if not the chattering classes.

If only they'd wait for a year, two or three,
my book would be published, they could have little me!
I'd yield to all pressures and sing as I'm told,
and when the heat's on, I'd be cautious not bold.
Though I offer this warning, if faced with rank failure,
I'd gird up my loins, bugger off to Australia.

So here then is my parting shot
to fit all kinds of function;
whatever it is they want – or not –
I'll do it without compunction.

LET.........BE..........AT THIS TIME OF
    GREAT................
THE ....IS..........; ....WITH ALL
    YOUR...............

Port Isaac and London
17-20th April, 1999

ALONE 4.00 AM

To lie awake
so late – or early –
no shields of sound
or hurly-burly,

nor love to take
some comfort from;
I'm old and tired
and sleep won't come.

Kentish Town
3rd June 1999

A DEFINITIVE NON-STATEMENT 5.00 A.M.

In my life now,
God in all his glory
is a non-starter.

Neither my ancestral
rabbinic roots
nor the richness
of the risen Christ,
the wise Buddha,
no remote sense
of cosmic purpose,
or first-cause arguments
move me.

It is as it is
because it is;
I have no problems
with all of that.

Good and evil,
pain and pleasure,
love and hate
and life and death,
even the best and worst
of all possible worlds,
here, there or (who knows)
anywhere,
none of these
disconcerts, elevates
or reduces me.

What is more – or less –
I feel and see
no spiritual dimensions,
no joyous surprises
around the next corner,
no tortured or beguiling
landscapes over the human horizon.

Personal agonies apart,
I am- for a short time –
what I am.

Do I wish it were not so?

Kentish Town
3rd June 1999

MIND UNSET

Brought on by a surfeit of Ireland, the Balkans and
memory lapses.

For Penny and Simon, Imogen and Pete.

When young and full of crap, I always knew
That what I said was wise beyond retort.
An ancient now, I take a different view;
I'm nothing like as clever as I thought.

For safety's sake, I play it from the sidelines,
I watch the others battle; let them squirm.
I never reach conclusions, just form guidelines,
my judgement's balanced but my mind's not firm.

As you get old, you learn a trick or two,
how to seem wise, be cunning, not get caught.
You still try hard at times to think things through
yet if you fail, accept it; don't feel fraught.

So life's no picnic – nevertheless it's true
most others are as vulnerable as you.

Kentish Town
16 July 1999

TRANTER REUBEN

A seminal figure – perhaps –
both in John Betjeman's 'Dorset' and
Thomas Hardy's 'Friends Beyond'.

Tranter Reuben (yes, Tranter Reuben!)
lies in Mellstock Churchyard now;
but who there keeps him company
in deepest Dorset's Eng. Lit. past,
those of the pen or of the plough?

Betjeman and Hardy used him,
a literary device, no worse.
J.B.'s cast was not in malice,
just, he claims, in euphony,
and Tranter's there in every verse,

preceding Eliot, Edith Sitwell,
H.G. Wells and Edna Best,
and lesser lights like Brian Howard,
Harold Acton (even T. Hardy),
a wicked list for a rural fest.

Hardy, earlier, in fine whimsy
summoned his friends from the grave to come
'We've no wish to hear the tidings',
'Death gave us all we possess.'
Only Tranter Reuben's dumb.

The squire, the farmer, William Dewy,
Lady Susan, John and Ned;

all the boys and girls have views
except T.R. who lineless sits.
What was he like ere he was dead?

Grand old Tranter, strong and silent,
(isn't it the oddest thing,
that he lives on in jesting verses
by two most distinguished poets)
in life unknown, in death a king.

A man whose great days came post-mortem,
a Dorset giant (don't wonder how).
Now immortal, Tranter Reuben,
dear Tranter Reuben, ah Tranter Reuben,
glows in Mellstock churchyard now.

Port Isaac
21st July 1999

NB. Being far from my reference books, I have not been able to check whether Mellstock – and even Tranter Reuben – are real, or imagined by T.H., shortly followed by J.B. Nor shall I bother – it doesn't matter!

NB2. But serendipity being what it is, I immediately came across an illustration and description in 'The Trombonist' of the Mellstock Band, fresh from its triumph in BBC TV's "Pride and Prejudice" and 'playing and singing lusty music of the type popular in West Country villages since the eighteenth century.' I await a telephone call from Tranter Reuben's grand-daughter.

NB3. Research is better still. Phil Humphries, who runs the Mellstock Band, says that like Hardy, they used his invention 'Mellstock'. The real village is called Stinsford. I shall never get that telephone call!

MY GARDEN

For Toby Wain who did it for me.

Song

    To garden is a loathesome task, God knows,
    those weeding, pruning, burning, watering skills
    that others cherish; me – it almost kills,
    it ruins your back and messes up your clothes.

Only a Lawn

    Lovely to sit on,
    delightful to mow,
    the only technique
    this idler can show;
    for guilt still empowers
    in a desperate way.
    My last ditch defence
    keeps the jungle at bay.

The Dream

    If I were rich, I'd settle for
    a chauffeur-driven motor,
    a chef to serve my parties
    with my Mouton-Rothschild quota.

    But above all these I'd welcome
    a gardening professional,
    I wouldn't lift a finger,
    (I'd admit in the confessional).

No other amanuensis
could give me such a thrill;
he'd plan and plant and dig and reap;
I'd smile, applaud, sit still.

For the devil's in the detail
so let him ponder hard on
what flowers and fruit I ought to have
to make my perfect garden.

A Cultivated Plot

And thus delegating,
I'd adore my green space,
the proudest non-gardener
in the whole human race.

30/31 July 1999
Port Isaac

EARLIER AND LATER

After an enchanting evening at the Saint Endellion Festival
('Façade' by Edith Sitwell and William Walton)
29th July 1999

Lady Walton and Richard Baker read;   *'Still falls the rain'*
Richard Hickox conducted.   Edith Sitwell

A memorable jolly occasion,
Susana Walton twinkled and shone
and the Richards Baker and Hickox
had a ball – didn't we all – what fun!

It's playful Twenties Edith,
stretching taller than a crane,
rhinoceros-glum, hippopotamus-glum;
true her rhymes and her beasts in the main

sound familiar. And she'll repeat some
several times before she's done.
Though no reason to be critical;
she too was having her fun.

But older Edith's sombre;
Christ bleeds, heart withers, men die.
Not fun at all while the rain still falls
from an alien murderous sky.

In the rose of her heart's dark passing
is our doom; time for us to remember
that the ball at which we danced in May
we're not asked to in November.

Port Isaac: St Endellion parish
29 July – 3 August 1999

ESKIMO KNELL

"Ours is an ice-house, ours is"
Variant on an early twentieth century street rhyme.

Daily life around an Inuit igloo
is dangerous whatever you do.
White bears pounce in the dark,
kayak fishing's no lark;
and it's freezing! I'm leaving, wouldn't you?

WORDS FAIL ME

Every now and then,
I'm shaken, caught short
by a phrase whose real meaning's
not quite what I thought

Sometimes or always?
My mind's locked in spasm,
vertigo on the edge
of a cerebral chasm.

Trapped without warning,
I reach for my pen,
every so often ....

....

every now and then?

Putney, Kentish Town
26/27/30th September 1999

"ONE DAY THEY'LL UNDERSTAND"

In memoriam
Emily Dickinson
Gerard Manley Hopkins
Enoch Soames

For most of us, this is our own true story,
a modest life, with precious little glory.
Would glory, though, be precious if it came?
One often pays a nasty price for fame,
or hopes of it thereafter, never knowing
which way – how hard – that wanton wind is blowing.
Composers, poets, generals versed in slaughter,
are their names carved in stone or writ on water?

If life's a one-time trip it doesn't much matter,
though you'll not know, your name might yet live on.
Be famous or content? Some choose the latter;
a safer place by far is staying anon.

But if you lust for praise and greatness till it hurts,
don't live too long, you might not like your just
   deserts.

4/5, 10 October 1999
Kentish Town/Putney

FACE VALUES

For Angela Landels, my favourite portrait painter

Faces look at me and say
"We know who we are today."
It must be true, I'd have no doubt
that what's inside is what looks out.

I recognize, but can't recall
detail in any face at all,
so every meeting somehow seems
like re-emergence from a dream.

You look hard at a face and ask
"What dangerous man or woman inside
deep behind those features hides?"
What secret fire under the mask

smoulders on for your eye to catch,
your fingers to follow with brush or pen,
expression, skin texture, head shape? Then,
will what you see and what's there match?

How near the truth dare a painter go
if a client is paying for an all-star show?
Is the sitter buying the right to know
that posterity views him in a rosy glow?

Faces still look at me and say
"We all know who we are today."
You see faces in a different way,
you screw down their image, then you play

with present and past, outside and in,
(a portrait's a kind of art-doctor's spin).
Wear your brave face while they bask
    in the light,
but Dorian Gray's lurking, not far out of sight.

October 1999

NOT YET TIME

Art is long
(though not forever).
Life's so short
that it's not clever

starting writing
verse too late;
soon some old fool
will slam the gate.

But art, like love,
is not past mending,
though both may pass
before our ending.

It's not yet time
for us to grieve.
Catch them quickly
lest they leave.

Port Isaac, November 1999

AFTERWORD

Born in Birmingham in 1933, Graham Tayar was educated at
King Edwards School, Birmingham, and Jesus College,
Cambridge. After teaching in Birmingham and then, for nearly
six years, in Addis Ababa, Ethiopia, he spent twenty-five years
as a BBC Radio producer and manager, mainly in London. He
also founded (in 1971), runs and plays piano in a traditional jazz
band, the Crouch End All Stars. Jewish – though non-observant
and non-believing – he is, by an accident of genes and
temperament, a reasonably sanguine person who does not suffer
from depression, even if some of the poems might suggest
otherwise.

PUBLICATIONS

Personality and Power, BBC Publications, 1973

Education at Home and Abroad, Routledge and Kegan Paul,
1974

Living Decisions, BBC Publications, 1973/1974

and various pamphlets, articles and poems.

PRODUCTIONS

Jazz Masters, Bruce Turner/Johnny Barnes, Cadillac Records,
1975

Sunday Best, Crouch End All Stars with Ian Christie, Jazzology,
1986

and many radio series and programmes.

Also from Smaller Sky Books:

William Cooper – Scenes From Death and Life

The final novel from one of post-war Britain's most respected and popular novelists.

> *...I suddenly realised that my gaze had been caught by two hundred 20 year old men and women, hair glistening from being washed, eyes bright with attention for what I was going to say, lips eager and rosy...something had come into the atmosphere which made me recall the favourite dictum of one of my colleagues: "Teaching is the most erotic of professions."*

Joe Lunn, the hero of William Cooper's "Scenes from Provincial Life", is now, in the 1980s, a novelist and teacher living in London with his young wife and two daughters. He is also a rather rebellious University lecturer whose mind is not always on his work...

Scenes From Death and Life, William Cooper's latest and last novel, is the funny and very moving account of those things which happen to us all, life, love, death and rebirth, all told in the unique style of one of Britain's most senior and popular writers.

William Cooper has been called the godfather of the Angry Young writers of the 1950s: Amis and Braine, Sillitoe and Wain. "Scenes from Provincial Life" may have influenced them all. But he has always seen himself as an utterly individual man and writer: 'You can't read a book by me and think it was by anybody else."

This book not only completes his "Scenes from" series; it completes William Cooper's entire life's work.

"...highly recommended..." PRIVATE EYE.

Price £7.99 in the United Kingdom.

ISBN 1 903100 00 3

To order this book, or any other titles from Smaller Sky Books, ask in your local bookshop, or write to Smaller Sky Books, 217 Woodstock Road, Oxford, UK OX2 7AD, enclosing a cheque or postal order for £7.99 plus £1.50 for package and posting.

Or telephone us on 07050 632277

Email: orderline@smallerskybooks.co.uk

Visit our website at www.smallerskybooks.co.uk *for the latest news on our catalogue and events, including live readings from Not Too Late For Loving by Graham Tayar.*

In the spring of 2000 Smaller Sky Books will be publishing a volume of Selected Poems by the late writer and critic, the former Oxford Professor of Poetry, John Wain.

This will be a major retrospective on one of the so-called 'Movement' poets, among whom were Philip Larkin, Donald Davie and Elizabeth Jennings. The book will be a selection of John Wain's verse going back to 1947 and including some previously unpublished poems. It will also include two chapters of his memoirs, entitled 'Earthtrack', which have never previously appeared.

For more information, or to reserve a copy, or to be placed on the Smaller Sky Books mailing list, please write to us at the above address, telephone or e-mail.